KA BX00 136304 9001

KT-371-848

Dun Laoghaire-Rathdown Libraries
DEANSGRANGE LIBRARY
Inv/07 : L631J   Price E6.23
Title: Over the rainbow
Class: J791.43 GAR

Over the Rainbow

The Story of
Judy Garland

Ann Jungman

Illustrated by Lynn Willey

BAINTE DEN STOC

WITHDRAWN FROM
DÚN LAOGHAIRE-RATHDOWN COUNTY
LIBRARY STOCK

Judy aged 17

OXFORD
UNIVERSITY PRESS

OXFORD
UNIVERSITY PRESS

Great Clarendon Street, Oxford OX2 6DP

Oxford University Press is a department of the University of Oxford.
It furthers the University's objective of excellence in research, scholarship,
and education by publishing worldwide in

Oxford New York

Auckland Bangkok Buenos Aires Cape Town Chennai
Dar es Salaam Delhi Hong Kong Istanbul Karachi Kolkata
Kuala Lumpur Madrid Melbourne Mexico City Mumbai Nairobi
São Paulo Shanghai Taipei Tokyo Toronto

Oxford is a registered trade mark of Oxford University Press
in the UK and in certain other countries

© Ann Jungman 2003

The moral rights of the author have been asserted
Database right Oxford University Press (maker)

First published 2003

All rights reserved. No part of this publication may be reproduced,
stored in a retrieval system, or transmitted, in any form or by any means,
without the prior permission in writing of Oxford University Press,
or as expressly permitted by law, or under terms agreed with the appropriate
reprographics rights organization. Enquiries concerning reproduction
outside the scope of the above should be sent to the Rights Department,
Oxford University Press, at the address above

You must not circulate this book in any other binding or cover
and you must impose this same condition on any acquirer

British Library Cataloguing in Publication Data

Data available

ISBN 0 19 919629 X

3 5 7 9 10 8 6 4

Mixed Pack (1 of 6 different titles): ISBN 0 19 919632 X
Class Pack (6 copies of 6 titles): ISBN 0 19 919631 1

Illustrated by Lynn Willey c/o J Martin & Artists
Cover photo by Sunset Boulevard/Sygma/Corbis UK Ltd.

Acknowledgements
p 1 Underwood & Underwood/Corbis UK Ltd.;
p 4 Bettmann/Corbis UK Ltd.; pp 4/5 Corel; p 5 Bettmann/Corbis
UK Ltd.; p 6 Rex Features; p 23 CinemaPhoto/Corbis UK Ltd.;
p 26 Corbis UK Ltd.; p 36 (top) Bettmann/Corbis UK Ltd.;
p 36 (bottom) Sunset Boulevard/Sygma/Corbis UK Ltd.;
p 37 Bettmann/Corbis UK Ltd.; p 42 Bettmann/Corbis UK Ltd.;
p 44 Bettmann/Corbis UK Ltd.; p 45 Hulton|Archive/Getty
Images; p 46 Bettmann/Corbis UK Ltd.; pp 46/47 Corel;
p 47 Bettmann/Corbis UK Ltd.

Printed in China

Contents

Story Introduction

A star is born

The picture on the front of this book is the image of Judy Garland that most people recognise. It is from ***The Wizard of Oz***, the film that made her a star.

However, what most people *don't* know is that the real life Judy, born Frances Gumm, had a difficult and sometimes lonely life both before and after she was famous. She was very close to her father who died when Judy/Frances was still very young. Her relationship with her mother was not a very good one, and this book will show how that 'shaped' the future for her.

1938: Judy with her mother

1

Baby

Baby Frances Gumm

Judy Garland was just two years old when she first stumbled on to the stage of her father's cinema. She sang "Jingle Bells".

"Get the kid off the stage," yelled someone.

However, she sang the song three times until her father took her off the stage to cheers. So began one of the most amazing careers in show business.

Judy's real name was Frances Gumm. She was known as "Baby" – the youngest of three daughters of Ethel and Frank Gumm. Ethel was sure that one of her children would become a big star.

"Oh, Frank! We've got to take Baby to Hollywood," cried Ethel.

"What's the hurry?" said Frank. "Let her grow up first. Fame can come later."

"Frank! I am taking her to Hollywood. And that is that."

Frances ran up to her parents.

"Baby, honey, you were great! We're so proud of you."

Frances buried her head in her father's lap.

"You've got something Baby," said Jinny, Frances' oldest sister.

"Yeah," agreed Susie, her other sister. "You finally found the star material you always wanted, Mom."

Ethel beamed. "We're going to sell up. We're all going to California! To Hollywood. Your sister is going to be a great star in the movies."

Six weeks later, the family set off in their old Ford. They needed to earn money while they travelled. So every night, the family performed in whichever small town they found themselves. It was 1925, before television, in the very early days of radio and films. Entertainment was hard to come by. Crowds would pack into the church hall to see whatever was on offer.

First Frank would sing. He had a good voice and played the guitar nicely. The crowd enjoyed that. Then the older girls, Jinny and Susie, would do a song and dance act, while Ethel played the piano. That went down well too. The crowd liked the youngsters.

After that Ethel would sing. And the crowd hated her. They would boo and throw things on stage. Frank and the family wanted to die of embarrassment.

The last act was Frances and her sisters. Then "Baby" had a small solo. The effect was always the same. The crowd cheered and called for more.

"When we get her to Hollywood, she'll make it big," smiled Ethel. Her own problems faded away, when she thought of her daughter's golden future.

On the Road

"At last," breathed Ethel, as they drove into Hollywood. "The Gumms have arrived!"

But Hollywood turned out to be a hard place.

The family could only afford one room. And the town was full of mothers who believed their children were wonderfully talented.

"Look at all those silly women and their sad kids," said Frank. "Let's just take our children home and forget about this."

"You go, if you want," answered Ethel. "But my Frances is special. Sooner or later, someone will see it."

So Ethel dressed little Frances up in an ugly, pink, frilly dress. And they joined the queues waiting to be discovered. Every night, Ethel would drag an exhausted Frances back to the one room they all shared.

"Listen, Ethel. I'm running out of money," Frank told his wife, firmly. "And the girls need a proper home."

"Yes, Momma," agreed the children. "Living in Hollywood is getting us nowhere."

"Do you want to leave here, too, Frances?" demanded Ethel.

"I want to be with my Daddy," Frances told her.

In the end, Frank used his last money to buy a small cinema in a desert town within driving distance of Hollywood.

Before they left, Ethel signed up all the girls with the Melin Kiddies Agency. This agency was supposed to find work for child performers. All the girls were offered badly paid work at tiny theatres. However, by law, the two older ones had to go to school and could only perform at the weekends.

Now Ethel put all her hopes on Frances. She dragged her from theatre to theatre, always hoping that some **talent scout** would be at that particular performance. Frances hated being away from her warm and loving father. But when she got on stage and started singing, somehow everything seemed all right. Audiences loved the plump, little girl singing her heart out. And Frances loved them for loving her.

She was very lonely a lot of the time. The other child performers were mostly older. She had no one to play with or talk to. Sometimes she felt desperate.

"Please, Momma, can we go home," she begged.

"Don't you want to be a star?" demanded Ethel.

The little girl shook her head.

But Ethel insisted that they keep travelling from theatre to theatre. Frances would perform and then she and Ethel would go back to some small, cheap hotel. Some nights, Frances would sob and sob.

"What's the matter?" snapped Ethel.

"I want my Daddy and I want my sisters," wept five-year-old Frances.

"Oh, so your mother isn't enough for you?" fumed Ethel. "Your mother who slaves to make you a star. If that's how you feel, you can stay here on your own. I'm off!"

"No, Momma," shrieked Frances, "Don't go, don't leave me! Please, Momma, don't leave me alone in this place. I'll be good! I'll stop crying."

But Ethel would walk out of the room, and slam the door, leaving Frances on her own. Some hours later, Ethel would return to find Frances shaking with fear.

"Promise Momma there will be no more 'I want my Daddy'," insisted Ethel.

"I promise, Momma," wept Frances.

Then Ethel would put her daughter on her knee and comfort her, knowing that she had won.

CHAPTER

3

Judy Garland

Then came the day that Frank had good news for Frances.

"I've bought a house just outside Hollywood. You and Momma can come home."

"Oh, Dad, is it really true? Can we live in our own house, like everyone else?"

"That's right, Baby."

"And I'll see you every day?"

"Of course," promised her father.

Frances burst into tears. Only this time, they were tears of joy.

After that, Frances lived at home.

"Can I go to school, Dad?" asked Frances.

"Sure you can," agreed Frank.

But Ethel had not given up her ideas of stardom for her daughters. All three were sent to Mrs Lawlor's School for Professional Students. This was a school in Hollywood for children who wanted to be actors.

"How do you like your school, Baby? Are you making friends?"

"Oh, yes, Daddy. There's this boy called Mickey."

"Mickey what?" asked Frank.

"Mickey Rooney. Dad, he's so talented, he can sing and dance. He is the funniest person you ever saw."

Mickey Rooney and Judy in 1940

Little did Frances know that she would star in lots of films with Mickey Rooney. They would become best friends, and he stood by her through thick and thin. And she certainly needed friends.

Her parents' marriage went from bad to worse. Ethel shouted at Frank all the time. Frances cried as she listened to their fights.

But Frank would hug his youngest daughter and try to comfort her.

"What can I get you, Frances, to make you a happy girl again?"

"A dog, Poppa! I would love a dog."

So Frank bought her a dog. Frances adored him. If only her parents could get on, life would be almost normal.

Then one day Ethel announced: "The **World Fair** is going to be held in Chicago. Everyone's going. And that's where we should be."

"Ethel!" protested Frank. "The kids are just getting settled. Don't drag them off again."

"I want to stay with Poppa," wailed Frances.

"Go and get packed," said Ethel in a frosty voice. "A star goes where the work is."

When they got to Chicago, Ethel decided to call her girls the Gumm Sisters.

"You can't call an act 'the Gumm Sisters'," she was told.

"Why not?" demanded Ethel. "That's their name."

"Lady, think about it. Gumm rhymes with dumb and crumb. Not good. Find another name for these lovely girls."

"I don't know what to call them. Give me a suggestion," said Ethel.

Chicago World Fair 1933

"Call them after the pianist over there. His name's Robert Garland. Call them the Garland Sisters."

"Do you like that?" Ethel asked her daughters, "The Garland Sisters?"

The two older girls nodded, "Fine Mom."

"Frances, do you like it?"

Frances looked round.

"Sorry Momma, I was listening to that lovely song he's playing."

"Do you want to be one of the Garland Sisters?"

Frances nodded. "But I'd like to be called Judy, after this terrific song."

"Judy Garland," said the manager. "Now, that is a great name. Yeah!"

And so little Frances Gumm became the legendary Judy Garland. Audiences loved her.

Ethel watched from the wings, thinking, "My girl is ready to storm Hollywood next!"

CHAPTER

4

Hollywood

When they got back home, Ethel took Judy round all the studios.

"My daughter sings like an angel," she would tell the studios.

"Lady, that girl is too short, too plump and too ordinary-looking," everyone told her.

"Just listen to her sing," Ethel insisted.

"That's not enough. In Hollywood, you have to *look* like an angel too."

Judy thought she would die as studio after studio rejected her.

Then, when Judy was was a young teenager, Roger Edens, a musician from the biggest of all the studios, Metro Goldwyn Meyer, rang up. He wanted Judy to come in for an audition. Judy was at home with her father. Wearing casual clothes, grey trousers and a white shirt, she was playing with her dog.

Frank called out of the window.

"Hey, Judes! Metro want you for an audition, right away."

"I've got to change, Dad," she cried.
"No time! My girl looks stunning."
"Mom will kill me when she hears."
"OK, honey. Change in the car!"
When Judy got to the studios, she sang: "Zing Went the Strings of my Heart". Everyone listened in stunned silence. No one could believe that such a young girl could sing with such a tremendous voice, so packed with feeling.

"Get Mr Meyer," cried Roger Edens, "He's got to hear this kid! She's great! She's unbelievable."

So the great Louis B. Meyer, the most powerful man in Hollywood, came to hear little Judy sing. When she finished, he clapped.

"She's no beauty," he said. "But she looks nice. She looks like the girl next door. I can use her."

So eventually Judy was signed with
Metro Goldwyn Meyer. She was
fourteen. Ethel's dream was coming
true. But not quite yet.

Judy was signed on by a studio, but
she didn't make films. Instead, they
sent her to sing at the grand parties
the famous stars gave.

One evening, Judy was booked to
sing on the radio. Her beloved father,
Frank, had a bad earache.

"I won't go. I'll stay with Poppa."

"You'll do no such thing," snapped Ethel.

"It's OK honey. You go and I'll hear you on the radio. I'll be fine."

"I'll only be singing for you, Poppa."

That evening, Judy sang her heart out for her father. But that night, Frank died, very suddenly.

For months, Judy cried herself to sleep every night. Now, there was no one to defend her against her mother's huge ambitions.

Every day, Judy went to the studio school. She liked school and loved being with her old friend, Mickey Rooney.

CHAPTER

5

Wizard of Oz

One morning, Roger Edens asked to see Judy.

"The boss has just bought the rights to *The Wizard of Oz*. It's going to be the biggest musical ever. I think you'd be great as Dorothy."

"Oh, Mr Edens! I'd love to play that part."

But Louis B. Meyer told her, "You're not right Judy. You're too old. Dorothy is 10 and you're 16 and plump with it."

Judy was devastated. Roger Edens comforted her, "Believe me, they won't find anyone else with a voice like yours. Be patient."

Weeks later, Louis B. Meyer called for Judy. "OK," he told her. "You can have the part. But you must halve your weight."

For weeks, Judy ate nothing but chicken soup. Then the studio put her in tight corsets. But she still didn't look like a ten year old.

"Put the girl on slimming pills," insisted the studio head.

So Judy was put on slimming pills. The weight fell off her – but now she could not sleep.

"Give her sleeping pills," said the studio.

So Judy was given sleeping pills. But she had to be in the studio at five in the morning. And she could not wake up.

"Give her pep-up pills," said the studio.

So much against her will, Judy was put on pills. They were to haunt her for the rest of her life.

In spite of the corsets and the pills, Judy was happy. She loved playing Dorothy, the girl who finds herself on the yellow brick road, looking for the Wizard of Oz to help her get home to Kansas. No money was spared to make it the most spectacular film, ever. The sets were amazing. There were thousands of extras. And it had some great songs.

Now everyone was interested in Judy. Every day, journalists and photographers came to the studios to interview her. Her co-stars, playing the Cowardly Lion, the Tin Man and the Scarecrow were jealous of the attention she was getting. They made life as difficult for her as they could.

Margaret Hamilton and Judy Garland in The Wizard of Oz, 1939

The only person who helped Judy was the actress who played the Wicked Witch of the West, Margaret Hamilton.

When the studio bosses saw the film, they were delighted. But they didn't like one of the songs.

"Let's leave out "Somewhere, Over the Rainbow", said one. "It doesn't have a good tune."

"I agree," said another, "No one will like it."

Cast members pose by a giant promotional poster for The Wizard of Oz

Judy and Roger Edens had to fight hard for their favourite song. At last, it was left in. But only when the bosses were sure that everyone liked it.

And they did like it. They liked the whole film. It was the most successful film ever and Judy as Dorothy was a mega star.

From rising star...

The film is now a classic. Maybe Dorothy's search for happiness rang a bell for Judy Garland. She put her whole soul into a part for which she will always be remembered. As for "Somewhere Over the Rainbow", it became a classic too. It is one of the most popular songs ever. And it will always remind people of a timeless Judy Garland.

... to the best there is!

Young Judy
on a pony

Judy Garland has been described as looking very much like "the girl next door". This means that, compared to many of her fellow performers, it was thought Judy was pretty, but not beautiful. What do you think?

As a little girl, she was pushed into a very competitive world. She was told she was too plump. This, and the fact that at 16 years old she was playing the part of a 10 year old in *The Wizard of Oz* pushed Judy into unhealthy habits for life.

46

13-year-old
Judy having
some fun!

Her need to take pills to stay slim, her need to take more pills to help her sleep, and then more pills to wake her up again were common practices at the time. It was hard for Judy to stop all this. But the fact remains – she was a very talented and extraordinary person.

Index

Glossary

Andy Hardy Judy Garland began her acting career in the film series of this name in 1935

Talent Scout a person whose job it is to discover and recruit people with talent or particular skills

Wizard of Oz Judy Garland became an acting star when she performed in this film in 1939

World Fair This international showpiece was held in Chicago in 1933, and was called "A Century of Progress". It was a huge fair!